make

table runners

10 Delicious Quilts to Sew

C&T PUBLISHING

Text, photography, and artwork copyright © 2016 by C&T Publishing, Inc.

Publisher: Amy Marson

Creative Director: Gailen Runge

Project Editor: Alice Mace Nakanishi

Compiler: Lindsay Conner

Cover/Book Designer: April Mostek

Page Layout Artist: Casey Dukes

Production Coordinator: Zinnia Heinzmann

Photography by Diane Pedersen, Christina Carty-Francis, Luke Mulks, and Nissa Brehmer, of C&T Publishing, unless otherwise noted

For further information and similar projects, see the book listed after each artist's bio.

Published by C&T Publishing, Inc., P.O. Box 1456, Lafayette, CA 94549

Printed in China

10 9 8 7 6 5 4 3 2 1

Contents

10 TABLE RUNNERS

Star of the Picnic Table Topper

Sally Bell

FINISHED TABLE TOPPER:
27½" diameter

FINISHED BLOCK:
3" Friendship Star block

Designed by Sally Bell; pieced
and quilted by Marie Lanier

SALLY BELL (on the left) is the sister, long-time collaborator, and partner with Susan Maw for Maw-Bell Designs, specializing in patterns for quilts, children's clothing, and accessories. Sally lives in Montana, in the state's Bitterroot Valley.

WEBSITE: maw-belldesigns.com

This project originally appeared in *Summer at the Lake Quilts* by Susan Maw and Sally Bell, available from C&T Publishing.

Our Star of the Picnic Table Topper is the perfect size to show off that beautiful bouquet of flowers you picked on your mountain hike. We use one white fabric, four reds, and four blues to give it a scrappy look.

Materials

REDS: ⅛ yard each of 4 different fabrics

BLUES: ⅛ yard each of 4 different fabrics

WHITE: ⅔ yard

BINDING: ½ yard (cut on bias)

BACKING: 1 yard

BATTING: 36″ × 36″

Cutting

Use patterns A and Ar (page 30) as indicated.

REDS

Cut 5 strips 1½″ × width of fabric; subcut into 120 squares 1½″ × 1½″.

Cut 3 strips 1⅞″ × width of fabric; subcut into 60 squares 1⅞″ × 1⅞″ for half-square triangle units.

BLUES

Cut 24 of pattern A.

Cut 24 of pattern Ar.

WHITE

Cut 2 strips 1½″ × width of fabric; subcut into 30 squares 1½″ × 1½″.

Cut 3 strips 1⅞″ × width of fabric; subcut into 60 squares 1⅞″ × 1⅞″ for half-square triangle units.

Cut 14 of pattern A.

Cut 14 of pattern Ar.

Cut 1 strip 3½″ × width of fabric; subcut into 7 rectangles 3½″ × 5⅝″.

BINDING

Approximately 100″, 1½″ wide of continuous bias binding

Photo by Jesse Maw

Block Assembly

Follow the arrows for pressing direction.

1. Draw a diagonal line across the back of the light square and place it on the dark square, right sides together.

2. Sew ¼″ from each side of the diagonal line.

3. Cut the squares apart on the center line. You will have 2 half-square triangle units. Press toward the dark fabric.

4. Use the 1⅞″ × 1⅞″ red and white squares to piece 120 half-square triangle units 1″ finished size.

FRIENDSHIP STAR BLOCK

Unit A

Unit B

Unit C

Sew Units A, B, and C together to form a Friendship Star block.

Friendship Star block. Make 30.

BLOCK 1

1. Work in a counterclockwise direction.

2. Sew a blue pattern A to one side of the Friendship Star block.

3. Sew a white pattern A to the adjoining side of the Friendship Star block.

4. Sew a blue pattern A to the third adjoining side of the Friendship Star block. Make 6.

Block 1. Make 6.

BLOCK 1A

1. Repeat Block 1, Steps 1–3.

2. Sew a white pattern A to the fourth side of the Friendship Star block. Make 4.

Block 1a. Make 4.

BLOCK 2

1. Work in a clockwise direction.

2. Sew a blue pattern Ar to one side of the Friendship Star block.

3. Sew a white pattern Ar to the adjoining side of the Friendship Star block.

4. Sew a blue pattern Ar to the third adjoining side of the Friendship Star block. Make 6.

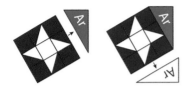

Block 2. Make 6.

BLOCK 2A

1. Repeat Block 2, Steps 1–3.

2. Sew a white pattern Ar to the fourth side of the Friendship Star block. Make 4.

Block 2a. Make 4.

Assembly

Refer to the table topper assembly diagram. Follow the arrows for pressing direction.

1. Sew the blocks together into rows as indicated.

2. Sew the rows together as indicated, matching the corners of the Friendship Star blocks. Press all the row seams toward the bottom.

Binding

Use a single-thickness binding when applying it to scallops or curved quilt edges. Cut bias strips 1½" wide. Press one edge under ¼". Pin the unpressed edge of the binding to the edge of the quilt top, right sides together and edges aligned. Stitch, easing the binding at the outer curves without stretching and pivoting at the inner curves. Clip the seam allowances at the innermost point. Fold the pressed-under edge over the back of the quilt and hand stitch down.

Table topper assembly

Clamshell Garden Runner

Wendy Williams

Photo by John Doughty | Spy Photography

I have always loved the idea of doing clamshells, but I know I will never get around to doing a whole quilt with them. I used them for the garden bed in this quilt, giving the shells a contemporary feeling by using modern fabrics and wool. The flower stems are swaying in the breeze, adding movement to the design. Search through your stash to find small flower and circle motifs for the flower centers. Audition different background fabrics to give a different look to your design.

WENDY WILLIAMS began her career as a teacher of fashion, expanding to teach patchwork and quilting. She is a prolific designer of quilts, housewares, clothing, and bags. She started her pattern business, Flying Fish Kits, by selling patterns and kits online. Kathy lives near Sydney, Australia.

WEBSITE: flyingfishkits.com.au/kits

This project originally appeared in *Wild Blooms & Colorful Creatures* by Wendy Williams, available from C&T Publishing.

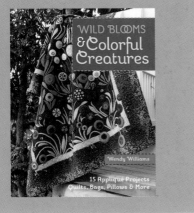

Materials

Yardage is based on 44"- (112 cm-) wide fabric, unless otherwise noted.

CREAM WORD PRINT: ½ yard (45 cm) for background

BRIGHT WITH DOTS: ¼ yard (25 cm) for Border 1

BRIGHT PRINTS: 25–28 pieces 3½" × 10"–12" (9 cm × 25 cm–30 cm) for Border 2 (These can be from your scrap basket.)

CIRCLE PRINTS: 37 motifs for flower centers

COTTON PRINTS AND WOOL FELT: 4" × 8" (10 cm × 20 cm) pieces in a variety of greens for clamshells (These can be from your scrap basket.)

WOOL FELT: 12–14 squares 8" × 8" (20 cm × 20 cm) in a variety of bright colors

GREEN WOOL FELT: 3 squares 10" × 10" (25 cm × 25 cm) of 3 different greens

3" CLAMSHELL PAPERS: 1 packet of at least 29 pieces, or make your own using the clamshell pattern (page 30)

BACKING: 1½ yards (1.4 m)

BINDING: ⅜ yard (35 cm)

BATTING: 25" × 54" (64 cm × 138 cm)

PERLE COTTON THREADS: size 8 in a variety of colors, including green

GLUE STICK

Cutting

CREAM PRINT: Cut 1 piece 13½" × 42½".

CIRCLE PRINTS: Cut approximately 37 circles, 1"–2½" in diameter, with a ¼" seam allowance.

BORDER 1: Cut 3 strips 1½" × width of fabric; subcut 2 strips 1½" × 15½" and use the remaining to piece 2 strips 1½" × 42½".

BORDER 2: Cut approximately 85 pieces of bright prints in various sizes: 2" × 3½", 2½" × 3½", and 3" × 3½".

BINDING· Cut binding as needed for your preferred binding style.

APPLIQUÉ PIECES
Copy the appliqué patterns (page 30). The patterns give you the shapes to cut, and the pattern pieces show suggested stitching.

Note: *For cotton fabrics, trace around the freezer paper and cut out with a ¼" seam allowance for the flower centers. However, for the clamshells, allow ⅜". Follow the special instructions for seam allowances on the wool clamshell pieces.*

1. Trace the appliqué patterns onto the dull (paper) side of freezer paper and cut on the drawn lines.

2. Press the freezer-paper templates onto the right side of the appropriate felt or fabric.

3. Cut out all the appliqué pieces. Refer as needed to the following suggestions for fabric for the appliqué pieces.

Green felt: Cut a number of leaves (mine has 21) from the 3 colors of green felt. Use the pattern as a guide or simply cut them freehand. Use a rotary cutter to cut a variety of ¼" strips for the stems.

Clamshell fabrics: Cut 29 clamshells from cotton or wool. When cutting from cotton, allow a ⅜" seam allowance around the papers. When cutting from wool felt, you do not need to allow a seam allowance around the top curved edge, but do allow a ⅜" seam allowance around the papers on the lower sections.

Cotton fabric

For cotton, allow ⅜" allowance all around.

Wool felt

For wool, allow ⅜" allowance around bottom portion only.

Prepare the Background

Use a chalk pencil or iron-out marking pen to mark a line 3" from the lower edge of the background 13½" × 42½" piece. Mark the center along this line.

Appliqué

Note: *I like to stitch as much of the appliqué as I can before I apply it to the background.*

CLAMSHELLS

1. To prepare the cotton clamshells, apply a line of glue along the top, curved edge of the clamshell papers. Finger-press the cotton clamshells over the curved edge. Try to keep the edge smooth with no bumps. Press.

2. Remove the papers and carefully re-press the clamshells.

3. Place the clamshell papers on the front of the clam-shells and mark the points on the sides of the clamshell where the paper ends, as shown.

4. Arrange 14 clamshells on the background along the line, with the top edge of the clamshell touching the line. Starting from the center and working out toward the sides, position the clamshells so that the marked side points touch each other. Be sure to maintain the ¼″ seam allowance at each end of the background. Pin the clamshells in place.

5. Refer to the project photo (page 7) to arrange the lower row of 15 clamshells beneath the top row. The top curve of the lower row should touch the points on the upper row, the side points on the lower row should meet, and the bottom row of clamshells should cover the raw edges of the clamshells in the row above. Pin the lower row of clamshells in place. (The points of the clamshells on the lower row will extend beyond the edge of the fabric.)

6. Tack the top row of clamshells to the background. Do not finalize the stitching on the top row of clamshells yet.

7. Stitch the lower row of clamshells to the background—use perle cotton thread and a small running stitch close to the top curved edge on the cotton clamshells and a whipstitch on the felt. Trim the lower row of clamshells even with the edge of the background fabric.

Glue fabric over paper.

Mark points.

Mark points where paper ends.

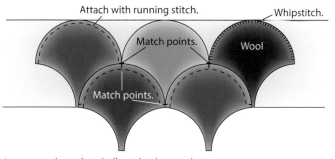

Arrange and pin clamshells on background.

FLOWERS

Photo by John Doughty | Spy Photography

1. Needle-turn appliqué the dotted flower circles to a piece of bright wool felt. Stitch with perle cotton and a running stitch close to the folded edge.

Felt

Cotton

Needle-turn cotton fabric onto felt.

2. Cut out the felt circles, keeping a ³⁄₈″–½″ edge around the flower fabric. (The circles don't need to be perfect; in fact, I think they look more organic if they are slightly uneven and not perfect.) You can make the flowers as small or as large as you like.

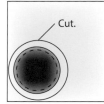

Cut.

Cut out circle.

3. Layer a circle on top of another piece of felt, and use a running stitch close to the edge to secure it. Cut out the new felt circle with a ³/₈″ edge around the stitch lines. Repeat.

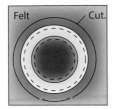

Stitch circle onto another piece of felt.

BACKGROUND SHAPES

Arrange all the appliqué pieces on to the background, using the project photo as a guide for placement.

1. Arrange the flowers and leaves on the background, moving them around until you are happy with the color placement.

2. Pin the flowers and leaves in place with appliqué pins.

3. Arrange the stems so they come from the flowers to the top of the clamshell border. Cut the stems to size and, if necessary, clip the tacking on the clamshells to allow the stems to tuck underneath. When you are happy with the stem placement, pin them in place.

4. Add some more leaves to complete the design.

5. Appliqué the flowers in place with a backstitch and a variety of colors of perle cotton thread.

6. Stitch the stems in place with small running stitches in green perle cotton thread.

7. Stitch the leaves in place with small whipstitches in green perle cotton thread.

8. Finish stitching the top row of clamshells to the background.

9. Trim the center to straighten up the edges. The center piece should measure 42½″ × 13½″, including seam allowances.

Add the Borders

Seam allowances are ¼″.

BORDER 1

1. Stitch the 1½″ × 42½″ border 1 strips to the top and bottom of the runner. Press the seams toward the border.

2. Stitch the 1½″ × 15½″ border 1 strips to the sides of the runner. Press the seams toward the border.

BORDER 2

1. Randomly stitch the bright print 2″ × 3½″, 2½″ × 3½″, and 3″ × 3½″ border 2 pieces together into a strip at least 132″ long. Press the seams.

2. Cut the long pieced strip to yield 2 strips 3½″ × 50½″ for the top and bottom and 2 strips 3½″ × 15½″ for the sides.

3. Stitch a 3½″ × 15½″ strip to each side, pressing the seams toward border 1. Stitch the 3½″ × 50½″ strips to the top and bottom and press the seams toward border 1.

Table runner assembly

Finish

1. Layer, baste, and quilt as desired.

2. Use your preferred method to bind the edges.

Pinwheel Table Runner

Kim Schaefer

FINISHED TABLE RUNNER:
23″ × 57″

FINISHED BLOCK: 8″ × 8″

Brighten your table with this cheerful pinwheel table runner in the classic color combination of red and white.

Quilted by Julie Karasek of Patched Works, Inc.

KIM SCHAEFER is a best-selling author and the founder of Little Quilt Company, which is known for its small, fun-to-make quilting patterns. A fabric designer with Andover Fabrics, Kim lives in Southeastern Wisconsin.

WEBSITE: littlequiltcompany.com

This project originally appeared in *Flower Festival* by Kim Schaefer, available from C&T Publishing.

Materials

ASSORTED LIGHTS: 1 yard total for flower appliqué block backgrounds and pinwheel blocks

ASSORTED REDS: 1¼ yards total for pinwheel blocks and flower appliqué pieces

ADDITIONAL FABRIC: 2 yards for backing and binding

PAPER-BACKED FUSIBLE WEB: ¾ yard

BATTING: 26″ × 61″

Cutting

ASSORTED LIGHTS

Cut 5 squares 8½″ × 8½″ for the flower appliqué block backgrounds.

Cut 16 squares 4⅞″ × 4⅞″ for the pinwheel blocks. Cut the squares once diagonally for a total of 32 triangles.

ASSORTED REDS

Cut 16 squares 4⅞″ × 4⅞″ from the assorted reds for the pinwheel blocks. Cut the squares once diagonally for a total of 32 triangles.

Cut squares once diagonally.

Appliqué

1. Using the pattern (page 31), cut out 5 each of the flower appliqué pieces 1, 2, and 3.

2. Appliqué the appropriate pieces onto each background, using paper-backed fusible web.

Pinwheel Blocks

1. Sew a light triangle to a red triangle on the diagonal edges. Make 32 triangle squares. Press toward the red triangles.

Sew triangles. Make 32.

2. Piece the pinwheel blocks. Press. Make 8.

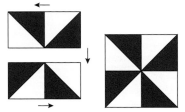

Piece pinwheel blocks. Make 8.

Putting It All Together

Arrange and sew the pinwheel blocks and the flower blocks into rows as shown. Press. Sew together the rows. Press.

Table runner assembly

Finishing

1. Layer the table runner with batting and backing, and baste or pin.

2. Quilt as desired, and bind.

Mardi Gras Runner

Jan Krentz

FINISHED TABLE RUNNER:
26″ × 52″

FINISHED BLOCK: 5½″ × 11½″

Try a Faux Diamond technique to create a fast, fun table runner from one colorful printed stripe. Add contrasting narrow borders and it's complete!

JAN KRENTZ is an award-winning, internationally recognized quilt instructor and designer. Jan's motivating presentations and workshops are packed with practical tips, techniques, and methods to ensure success. She is the author of several C&T books, a DVD, and the fast2cut rulers. Jan lives in Poway, California.

WEBSITE: jankrentz.com

This project originally appeared in *Quick Diamond Quilts & Beyond* by Jan Krentz, available from C&T Publishing.

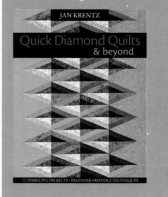

Materials and Cutting

Use a 6" × 12" ruler (see Cutting Rectangles for Faux Diamonds, below).

Yardage	For	Cutting
2 to 2½ yards multicolored stripe*	Blocks	Cut 16 rectangles, 6" × 12" (8 angled right, 8 angled left).
⅜ yard narrow black-and-white stripe	Border 1, long sides	Cut 3 strips, 1" × 42".
	Border 1, short sides	Cut 2 strips, 2" × 23½".
⅜ yard gold fabric	Border 2, long sides	Cut 3 strips, 2" × 42".
	Border 2, short sides	Cut 2 strips, 2" × 26½".
½ yard fabric	Binding	Cut 5 strips, 2¾" × 42".
1¾ yards fabric	Backing	
Batting: 32" × 58"		

* Yardage varies depending on the stripe width.

Cutting Rectangles for Faux Diamonds

Faux diamonds are made from striped fabrics, but they're not really diamonds at all. This slick effect is created by strategically cutting striped fabrics with a rectangular ruler—no diamonds at all! For ease, select a cutting ruler with a 1-to-2 ratio, such as 6" × 12".

1. Starch the fabrics before cutting them, to stabilize the edges during construction.

2. Fold the fabric, wrong sides together, aligning the stripes.

Align the stripes on both layers so they are running in the same direction, matching the same colors on the top and bottom layers.

3. Place the ruler on the fabric, aligning a stripe with the ¼" seamline at opposite corners (the corners of the finished-size rectangle). The stripe should not bisect the outer corner of the ruler. Cut through the double thickness, creating rectangles with diagonal stripes. When you cut correctly, you should have equal numbers of mirror-image rectangles from the 2 layers.

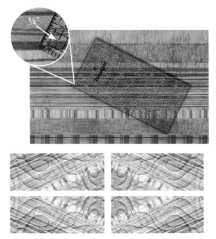

Equal quantities of mirror-image rectangles

Assembly

1. Arrange the rectangles on the design wall in 4 rows of 4 rectangles each. Move the pieces around until you are pleased with your design.

2. Sew the rectangles into rows. Press.

3. Sew the rows together. Press.

4. Piece the borders. Sew the 3 black-and-white 1" × 42" strips together end to end; cut into 2 strips, 1" × 46½". Sew the 3 gold 2" × 42" strips together end to end; cut into 2 strips, 2" × 49½".

5. Sew borders 1 and 2 to the quilt, adding the side borders first.

6. Layer the quilt top with the batting and backing, and baste. Quilt as desired. Bind.

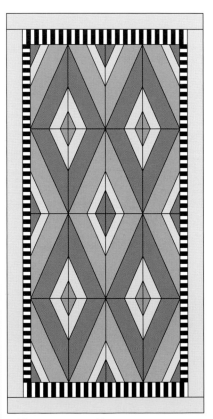

Table runner assembly

Going Green Table Runner

Kim Schaefer

FINISHED TABLE RUNNER:
20½″ × 60½″

FINISHED BLOCKS:
10″ × 10″, 5″ × 5″

Going green is easy when you whip up this table runner from a smorgasbord of greens. This scrappy runner is sure to brighten any tabletop.

Quilted by Diane Minkley

KIM SCHAEFER is a best-selling author and the founder of Little Quilt Company, which is known for its small, fun-to-make quilting patterns. A fabric designer with Andover Fabrics, Kim lives in Southeastern Wisconsin.

WEBSITE: littlequiltcompany.com

This project originally appeared in *Cozy Modern Quilts* by Kim Schaefer, available from C&T Publishing.

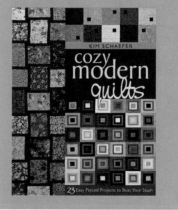

Materials

ASSORTED GREENS: 2 yards total for pieced blocks and pieced border

ADDITIONAL FABRIC: 2¼ yards for backing and binding

BATTING: 24″ × 64″

Cutting

ASSORTED GREENS: Cut for pieced blocks:

5 squares 6½″ × 6½″

20 rectangles 1½″ × 8½″

10 rectangles 1½″ × 6½″

10 rectangles 1½″ × 10½″

ASSORTED GREENS: Cut for pieced border blocks:

84 squares 1½″ × 1½″

56 rectangles 1½″ × 5½″

112 rectangles 1½″ × 3½″

Piecing

1. Piece the block as shown. Press. Make 5 blocks.

Step 1

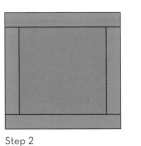

Step 2

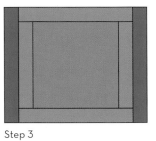

Step 3

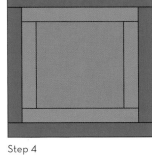

Step 4

2. Piece the border block as shown. Press. Make 28 blocks.

Step 1

Step 2

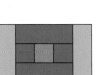

Step 3

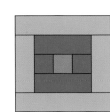

Step 4

Putting It All Together

1. Arrange and sew together 5 blocks to form the center of the table runner. Press.

2. Arrange and sew together 2 rows of 10 border blocks to make the side borders. Press.

3. Sew the 2 side borders to the runner top. Press toward the borders.

4. Arrange and sew together 2 rows of 4 border blocks to make the end borders. Press.

5. Sew the 2 end borders to the runner top. Press toward the borders.

Table runner assembly

Finishing

1. Layer the table runner top with batting and backing. Baste or pin.

2. Quilt as desired and bind.

Half-Circles Table Runner

Sweetwater

FINISHED TABLE RUNNER:
18½" × 37½"

Fused and appliquéd half-circles make this table runner a cinch to create. Try using this runner at breakfast—the colors in the appliqués and inner borders are so happy and energizing.

Designed and made by Sweetwater

SWEETWATER was founded in 2001 by Karla Eisenach and her two daughters, Lisa Burnett and Susan Kendrick. Located in Colorado, Sweetwater's simple yet sophisticated aesthetic infuses their many product lines, including fabric and quilt patterns for Moda.

WEBSITE: thesweetwaterco.com

This project originally appeared in *Sweetwater's Simple Home* by Karla Eisenach, Lisa Burnett, and Susan Kendrick, available from Stash Books.

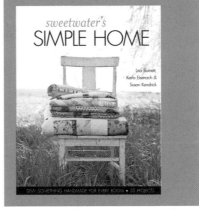

Photo by Farmhouse Creations, Inc.

Materials

FABRIC FOR BACKGROUND: 3 light neutral prints, ¼ yard each*

FABRIC FOR HALF-CIRCLE APPLIQUÉS: 3 different prints, ⅛ yard each

FABRIC FOR INNER BORDER: 3 different prints, each cut 1″ × width of fabric

FABRIC FOR OUTER BORDER: ⅓ yard light neutral print fabric*

PAPER-BACKED FUSIBLE WEB: ½ yard

EMBROIDERY FLOSS

BINDING: ⅓ yard

BACKING FABRIC: 26″ × 45″

BATTING: 26″ × 45″

We used very light tone-on-tone neutrals, but you could also use solid neutral fabric.

Background

1. Cut 2 pieces 18½″ × 5″ from each of the 3 neutral prints; there will be 6 total.

2. With the right sides together, sew the pieces together along the 18½″ sides, arranging the prints as shown. Press the seams to one side.

Fabric A
Fabric B
Fabric C
Fabric C
Fabric B
Fabric A

Appliqué

Use the pattern (page 30) as indicated.

1. Trace the circle and the cutting line from the pattern 18 times onto the paper side of the fusible web, leaving at least ½″ between the circles.

2. Cut out the circles, leaving a ¼″ margin around each. Iron 6 circles to the wrong side of each of the 3 appliqué prints, following the manufacturer's instructions.

3. Cut out the circles, and then cut each circle in half along the cutting line.

4. Peel off the paper backing and iron the half-circles to the center of each background strip, positioning the straight edges of the half-circles in the center of the strips as shown in the table runner assembly diagram.

5. Using 3 strands of embroidery floss, stitch a blanket stitch around the edges of each half-circle.

Borders

At each end of the table runner is an inner border pieced from 3 strips, and an outer border of neutral fabric.

1. Sew the print inner border strips together to make a strip set. Crosscut the strip set into 2 sections 18½″ long.

2. Sew 1 inner border strip set to each end of the table runner.

3. Cut 2 pieces 4″ × 18½″ from the outer border fabric and sew 1 piece to each end of the table runner.

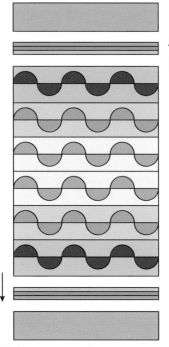

Table runner assembly

Finishing

For the binding, cut 4 strips 2¼″ × the width of the fabric; sew them together end to end, using diagonal seams, to make 1 long strip.

Layer, quilt, and bind the table runner as desired.

Two-Color Table Runner

Amanda Murphy

FINISHED TABLE RUNNER:
15" × 53½"

Pick two colors of the same value on opposite sides of the color wheel and experiment with making color vibrate! This can even work with two hues that are closer together on the color wheel as long as you stick with colors of similar value. It is also fun to make this project in two contrasting colors and let the quilting take center stage!

Pieced by Amanda Murphy; quilted by Deborah Norris

AMANDA MURPHY worked as a graphic designer and art director before she discovered quilting. She markets quilt patterns under the Amanda Murphy Designs label, and is a C&T author, a fabric designer, a Craftsy teacher, and a BERNINA quilting and longarm spokesperson. She lives in North Carolina.

WEBSITE: amandamurphydesign.com

This project originally appeared in *Color Essentials—Crisp and Vibrant Quilts* by Amanda Murphy, available from Stash Books.

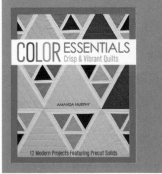

Table runner in vibrating colors

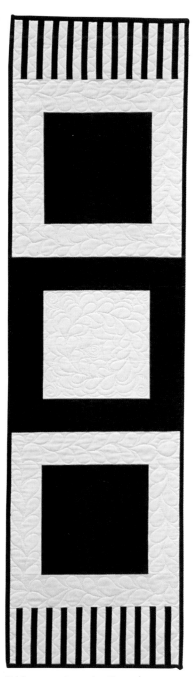

Table runner in contrasting colors

Materials

RUNNER FABRIC A: ³⁄₄ yard Kona 1011
Bahama Blue (or 1387 White)

RUNNER FABRIC B: ³⁄₄ yard Kona 192
Mango (or 1019 Black)

BACKING FABRIC: 1 yard Kona 1011
Bahama Blue (or 1387 White)

BINDING FABRIC: ¹⁄₃ yard Kona 192
Mango (or 1019 Black)

BATTING: 18″ × 57″ (I like Warm &
Natural batting by the Warm Company.)

PAPER-BACKED FUSIBLE TAPE: ¹⁄₄″ wide,
4 yards (I like Lite Steam-A-Seam 2.)

FUSIBLE BIAS TAPE MAKER: ¹⁄₂″ size
(*optional, but very helpful*)

Cutting

WOF = width of fabric

FABRIC A (BAHAMA BLUE)
Cut 3 strips 3¹⁄₄″ × WOF. Subcut
into 4 rectangles 3¹⁄₄″ × 9¹⁄₂″ and
4 rectangles 3¹⁄₄″ × 15″.

Cut 1 strip 5¹⁄₂″ × WOF. Subcut
into 2 rectangles 5¹⁄₂″ × 16″.

Cut 1 strip 9¹⁄₂″ × WOF. Subcut
into 1 square 9¹⁄₂″ × 9¹⁄₂″.

FABRIC B (MANGO)
Cut 2 strips 3¹⁄₄″ × WOF. Subcut
into 2 rectangles 3¹⁄₄″ × 9¹⁄₂″ and
2 rectangles 3¹⁄₄″ × 15″.

Cut 4 strips 1″ × WOF.

Cut 1 strip 9¹⁄₂″ × WOF. Subcut
into 2 squares 9¹⁄₂″ × 9¹⁄₂″.

BACKING FABRIC
Cut 2 strips 18″ × WOF.

BINDING FABRIC
Cut 4 strips 2¹⁄₄″ × WOF.

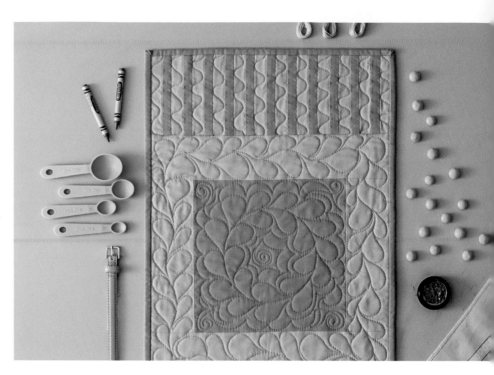

Block Assembly

Use a ¹⁄₄″ seam allowance unless noted otherwise.

1. Join fabric A rectangles 3¹⁄₄″ × 9¹⁄₂″
to the top and bottom of a fabric B
square 9¹⁄₂″ × 9¹⁄₂″. Join fabric A
rectangles 3¹⁄₄″ × 15″ to both sides of
this unit. Repeat to make a second unit.

2. Join fabric B rectangles 3¹⁄₄″ × 9¹⁄₂″
to the top and bottom of a fabric A
square 9¹⁄₂″ × 9¹⁄₂″. Join fabric B
rectangles 3¹⁄₄″ × 15″ to both sides of
this unit.

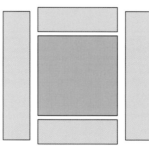

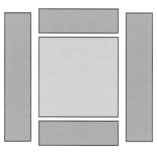

Border Assembly

1. Run 1" fabric B strips and ¼"-wide fusible tape through a fusible bias tape maker, following the product instructions. If you don't have a fusible bias tape maker, fold the fabric B strips lengthwise wrong sides together, so that the edges meet in the center of the strip. Fuse fusible tape to the wrong (folded in) side of the fabric B strips; *then* remove the paper backing.

2. Cut the strips into 22 segments 6½" in length.

3. Starting 1½" in from the short edge of a fabric A rectangle 5½" × 16", fuse 11 fabric B segments at even intervals ¾" apart, allowing the edges of the segments to overlap the fabric A rectangle.

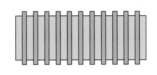

4. Secure the segments using an invisible hem stitch in matching thread.

5. Trim the edges of the segments flush with the border rectangle.

6. Centering the segments, trim the border to a rectangle 5½" × 15".

7. Repeat Steps 3–6 to make another border.

Runner Assembly

Following the assembly diagram, join the blocks and borders to form the runner.

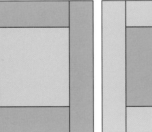
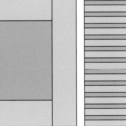

Finishing

1. Sew the short ends of the 2 backing fabric pieces together, press, and trim to a rectangle 18" × 57".

2. Layer the backing, batting, and runner top. Baste. Quilt as desired.

3. Bind the runner.

Spice Pink Table Runner

Karla Menaugh

FINISHED TABLE RUNNER:

12″ × 44″

Add some updated tradition to your table with our Spice Pink Table Runner *in the spiciest pinks you can find.*

Made by Karla Menaugh, quilted by Kelly Cline, 2013

KARLA MENAUGH is a journalist and editor with experience in both newspapers and public relations. With Barbara Brackman, she managed the Sunflower Pattern Cooperative, a successful quilt pattern company, for nearly ten years. Karla is skilled at machine quilting techniques, particularly machine appliqué, and teaches in guilds and shops. She lives near Louisville, Kentucky.

This project originally appeared in *Emporia Rose Appliqué Quilts* by Barbara Brackman and Karla Menaugh, available from C&T Publishing.

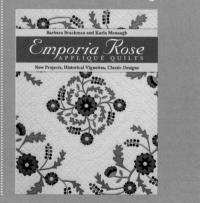

Materials and Cutting

Because the appliqué process tends to shrink the background slightly, the background is cut oversized. You will trim it to size after the appliqué is finished.

Before tracing and cutting appliqué shapes, refer to the photo as a guide to color placement.

Fabric	For	Cutting
1½ yards white	Background	1 rectangle 14″ × 47″
	Backing	1 rectangle 16″ × 50″
⅓ yard green	Long bias vine and large leaves	See pattern (page 32); photocopy at 200%.
1 fat quarter blue	Leaves and bias stems	
1 fat eighth blue-green	Tri-tipped leaves and bud stem	
6″ square each of 3 pinks, or use scraps	Flowers and buds	
5″ square yellow	Flower centers	
½ yard dark pink	Binding	4 strips 2½″ × width of fabric
18″ × 50″ batting		

Construction

1. Photocopy the appliqué pattern (page 32) at 200%.

2. Appliqué 3 repeats onto the white background fabric, flipping the direction of the vine in alternating sections.

MACHINE APPLIQUÉ

To use our machine appliqué technique, follow these steps.

1. Trace the enlarged pattern pieces, without seams, onto the shiny side of freezer paper.

2. Cut them out and iron them, shiny side down, to the wrong side of the fabric. Cut out, adding a ³⁄₁₆″ seam allowance.

3. Run a glue stick along the edge of the freezer paper and fold the fabric over the paper, leaving raw edges where any piece will be underneath another piece.

4. Position the appliqué pieces on the background and pin well. Or, better yet, baste with Roxanne Glue-Baste-It—a thin, white glue that comes in a plastic bottle with an applicator tip. Dot glue around the folded-under edges of the appliqué pieces and finger-press them into place on the background fabric.

This will eliminate the bumps and ridges caused by pins.

5. Stitch by machine using the variable overlock stitch.

6. Once everything is stitched down, soak or wash the entire piece in cold water and toss it in the dryer with a dry towel. When it's dry, carefully trim the underneath fabric (background fabric) to within ¼″ of the appliqué stitches. Remove the freezer paper and press from the wrong side. Trim the background or block to the correct size.

MAKING BIAS VINES

Our favorite method is to use a bias tape maker. These come in a variety of sizes that are useful for everything from ¼" stems to 1½" or 2" border vines. This project includes ⅜" and ½" bias vines.

1. Cut a bias strip twice as wide as the desired finished size. If you need to seam together strips to make a longer length than you can cut from your yardage, sew the seams diagonally to spread out the bulk of the seam allowance.

2. Clip an end of the strip at an angle and spray it lightly with spray starch or sizing.

3. Feed the angled end, right side of the fabric down, into the end of the bias tape maker. Pin the top of the strip to an ironing board.

4. Pull the bias tape maker along the bias strip, keeping the strip centered as it enters the tape maker.

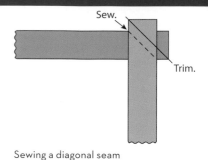

Sewing a Diagonal Seam

1. Place the ends of the strips right sides together with the top strip perpendicular to the bottom strip.

2. Sew a diagonal seam from the point where the strips cross at the top left to the point where they cross at the bottom right. Check to be sure the strip opens correctly, and then trim and press the seam allowance to the side.

Sewing a diagonal seam

5. Follow just behind the tape maker with a hot, dry iron. Pull the tape maker carefully so you won't stretch the bias strip. The tape maker will fold under both edges of the strip, and the hot iron will press them into place.

6. Allow the bias strip to cool for a few minutes before placing it on a block or border.

7. If you are not going to use the tape immediately, store it by winding it around a cardboard square or tube.

Use bias tape maker for bias vines.

QUILTING AND FINISHING

1. Trim the background to 12½" × 44½".

2. Quilt the background and stitch outside of each appliqué shape to puff up the appliqué. Typical Emporia quilting has few lines on the appliqué pieces.

3. Make and add the binding using the dark pink strips.

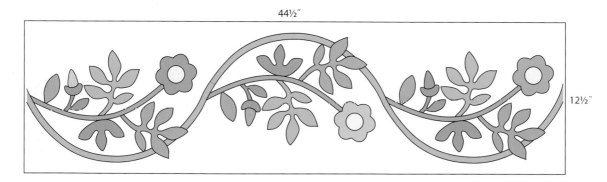

44½"

12½"

Twine Runner

Valori Wells

What a fun way to showcase a beautiful decorator print or one of your favorite fabrics in the larger sections of the table runner. The diagonal strip-piecing method adds interest between sections and around the edges.

VALORI WELLS is a professional quilter, author, fabric and pattern designer, painter, and photographer. She came into quilting through osmosis, having a mother who shared her love of quilting and who opened The Stitchin' Post in Sisters, Oregon, in 1974, now co-owned with Valori.

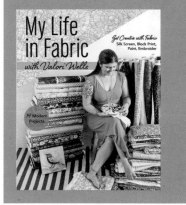

WEBSITE: valoriwells.com

This project originally appeared in *My Life in Fabric with Valori Wells*, available from Stash Books.

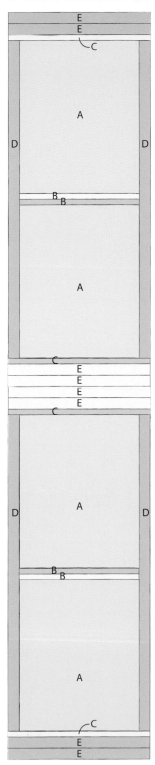

Table runner assembly

Materials

MAIN PRINT: ¾ yard (or more if it is a large print)

TWINE TRIM

PRINT FABRIC: ⅜ yard

SOLID FABRIC: ½ yard

PLAIN TRIM: ⅛ yard each of 1 light and 1 dark solid

BACKING: ⅞ yard

FLANNEL OR THIN BATTING: 1 yard

Cutting

WOF: width of fabric

MAIN PRINT
Cut 4 rectangles 12½″ × 15½″ (A), adjusting placement for large motifs.

TWINE TRIM (SOLID)
Cut 2 strips 1¾″ × WOF.
Cut 2 strips 2½″ × WOF.
Cut 2 strips 2″ × WOF.

TWINE TRIM (PRINT)
Cut 2 strips 1½″ × WOF.
Cut 2 strips 1¼″ × WOF.
Cut 1 strip 1″ × WOF.

PLAIN TRIM
Cut 2 strips 1″ × WOF from each of the light and dark solid fabrics.

Subcut each color into 2 strips 12½″ (B) and 2 strips 14½″ (C).

BACKING
Cut 1 rectangle 14½″ × 40″ and 1 rectangle 14½″ × 33″.

FLANNEL OR THIN BATTING
Cut 2 rectangles 14½″ × 36⋅⅛″.

Assembly

Seam allowances are ¼″ unless otherwise noted.

1. Arrange the 2 twine trim fabric strips, alternating a solid and a print. Stitch them together into 2 sets of 6 strips or one large set of all 12 strips. Press the seams in one direction.

2. Place a ruler at a 45° angle in the corner and cut along the edge of the ruler. Cut 1½″-wide strips across the pieced fabric. Join these strips together to create a long strip.

3. From the diagonal twine trim strip, cut:

4 strips 31½″ long (D)

8 strips 14½″ long (E)

4. Refer to the assembly diagram (page 25) and start sewing the sections together: A to B to B to A. Repeat for the other end of the runner. Press the seams in one direction. Sew D to each side of these units.

5. Sew C, E, E (checking color placement per diagram) to each end of the units. Press.

6. Sew the 2 units together. Press the seams in one direction.

IMPORTANT: The strips are cut on the bias so they can easily stretch. I suggest cutting as you go so that you don't handle them too much. And be careful not to pull them as you stitch. It's best to pin the seams before sewing.

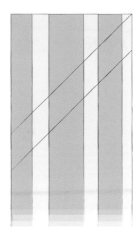

Cut at 45° angle.

Quilting and Finishing

1. Sew together the 2 backing pieces. Press the seam.

2. Sew together the 2 flannel or batting pieces by overlapping them ¼″ at the 14½″ edges and zigzag stitching.

Leave 4″ open

Sew around edges; clip corners.

3. Place the backing and runner right sides together and layer them on top of the flannel or batting. Pin around the edges.

4. Sew around the edges, leaving a 4″ opening on one side.

5. Clip the corners and trim the batting as needed. Turn the runner right side out. Press around the edges to flatten them. Hand stitch the opening shut.

6. For quilting, I echoed the design in the fabric, following the lines of the trees. Keeping it simple was the best approach to quilting this table runner.

Boardwalk Table Runner

Kim Schaefer

FINISHED BLOCK SIZE: 15″ × 15″

FINISHED TABLE RUNNER: 25½″ × 55½″

Bright, pieced blocks are surrounded by appliqué and a pieced jewel-toned border to give this runner a rich, lush look.

Quilted by Diane Minkley of Patched Works, Inc.

KIM SCHAEFER is a best-selling author and the founder of Little Quilt Company, which is known for its small, fun-to-make quilting patterns. A fabric designer with Andover Fabrics, Kim lives in Southeastern Wisconsin.

WEBSITE: littlequiltcompany.com

This project originally appeared in *Quilts from Textured Solids* by Kim Schaefer, available from C&T Publishing.

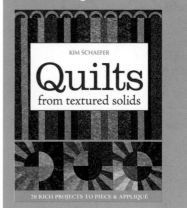

KIM SCHAEFER

Quilts
from textured solids

20 RICH PROJECTS TO PIECE & APPLIQUÉ

Materials

ASSORTED BRIGHTS (13): ⅛ yard each for pieced blocks

BLACK: ¾ yard for pieced blocks

RED: ¼ yard for pieced blocks

TAN: ⅓ yard for appliqué

ASSORTED DARKS: ¾ yard total for pieced border

PAPER-BACKED FUSIBLE WEB: ½ yard

ADDITIONAL FABRIC: 1¾ yards for backing and binding; ⅜ yard for binding if different from backing

BATTING: 30″ × 60″

Cutting

ASSORTED BRIGHTS: Cut 13 strips 1½″ × width of fabric for pieced blocks.

BLACK: Cut 12 squares 7″ × 7″ for pieced blocks.

ASSORTED DARKS: Cut 28 squares 5½″ × 5½″ for pieced border.

RED: Cut 6 strips 1½″ × 13½″ and 6 strips 1½″ × 15½″ for pieced blocks.

Piecing

1. Arrange and sew together 13 strips of assorted brights. Carefully press. The sewn strips should measure 13½″ × width of fabric.

Sew strips together.

2. Cut the sewn strips into 3 squares 13½″ × 13½″.

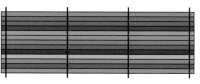

Cut 3 squares 13½″ × 13½″.

3. Using a light-colored fabric pencil, draw a diagonal line on the wrong side of each of the black 7″ × 7″ squares.

4. With right sides together, layer a black 7″ × 7″ square over 2 opposite corners of the pieced 13½″ × 13½″ square. Stitch the layered squares together on the drawn lines. Trim to ¼″ from the stitched lines. Press.

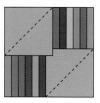 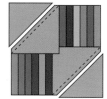

Stitch on drawn line.   Trim.

5. Repeat Step 4, placing a black 7″ × 7″ square over the remaining 2 corners of each pieced 13½″ × 13½″ square. Trim and press.

6. Sew a 1½″ × 13½″ strip to opposite sides of the pieced block. Press.

7. Sew the 2 strips 1½″ × 15½″ to the remaining sides of the pieced block. Press.

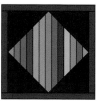

Piece blocks. Make 2.   Piece block. Make 1.

Appliqué

1. Use the patterns (page 30) to cut:

12 of pattern piece 1

24 of pattern piece 2

2. Appliqué the appropriate pieces to the blocks.

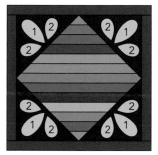

Appliqué blocks.

Putting It All Together

QUILT CENTER

Arrange and sew together the blocks in 1 row of 3 blocks. Press.

PIECED BORDER

1. Arrange and sew together 2 rows of 9 squares each for the 2 side borders. Press.

2. Sew the 2 side borders to the runner top. Press.

3. Arrange and sew together 2 rows of 5 squares each for the 2 end borders. Press.

4. Sew the 2 end borders to the runner top. Press.

Finishing

1. Layer the table runner with batting and backing. Baste or pin.

2. Quilt as desired, and bind.

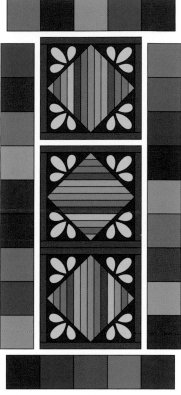

Table runner assembly

Patterns

Star of the Picnic Table Topper

(page 3)

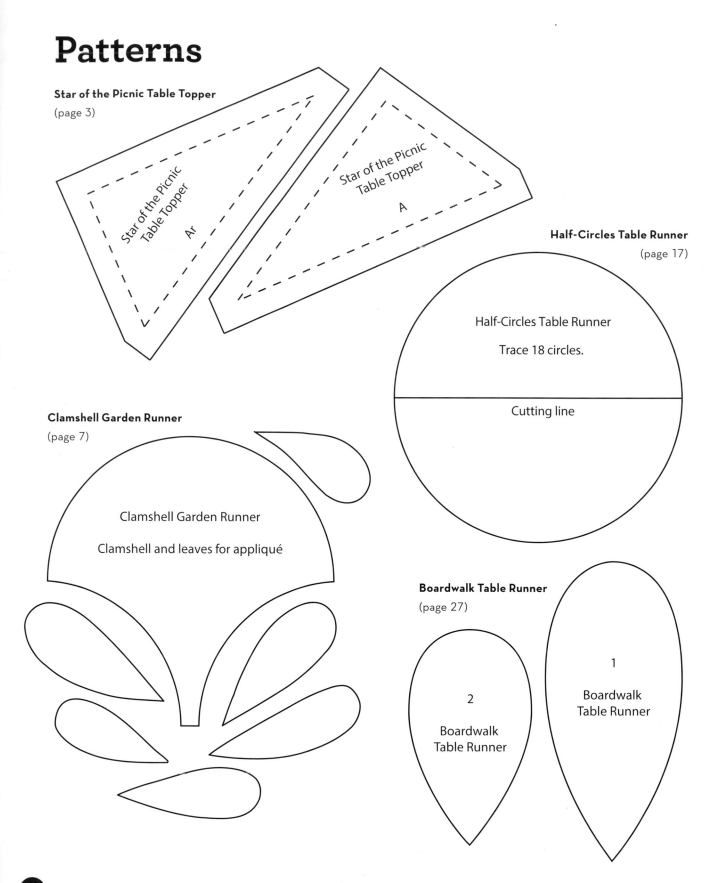

Star of the Picnic
Table Topper

Ar

Star of the Picnic
Table Topper

A

Half-Circles Table Runner

(page 17)

Half-Circles Table Runner

Trace 18 circles.

Cutting line

Clamshell Garden Runner

(page 7)

Clamshell Garden Runner

Clamshell and leaves for appliqué

Boardwalk Table Runner

(page 27)

1

Boardwalk
Table Runner

2

Boardwalk
Table Runner

Pinwheel Table Runner

(page 11)

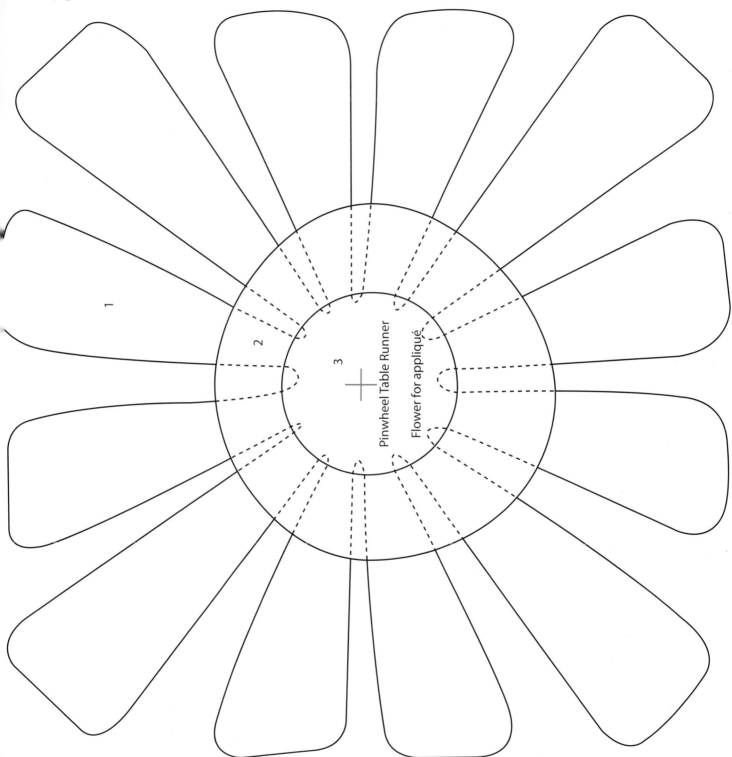

1

2

3

Pinwheel Table Runner

Flower for appliqué

Spice Pink Table Runner

(page 22)

Enlarge pattern 200%.

Cut 3.

Cut 3.

Cut 4 and 2 reversed.

Cut 3.

½" vine

Cut 2 and 1 reversed.

³⁄₈" stem

Cut 3.

Cut 3.

Cut 3.